MAD ALL OVER

The funniest Crystal Palace quotes... ever!

by Gordon Law

About the author

Gordon Law is an experienced journalist who has covered sport for the *South London Press*, the *Premier League* website, *Virgin Media* and national newspapers. He edits popular Palace fan site *Holmesdale.net* which he co-founded. Gordon has written other books on the Eagles: *Return to the Premier League* and *Premier Heroes,* which have chronicled the team's promotion and consolidation in the top flight.

Also available on Amazon or from the Palace club shop

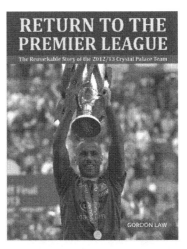

editor@holmesdale.net
www.holmesdale.net

Printed in the United States of America
ISBN-13: 978-1519335876
ISBN-10: 1519335873

Photos courtesy of: Ramzi Musallam, Gordon Law, Magnus Andersson, Peter Guntrip, Andy Roberts and Keith Gillard.

Contents

"That pigeonhole is off our back."

Photo: Ramzi Musallam

Introduction

Crystal Palace personalities have said the funniest, the strangest and the most downright bizarre things over the years.

While it's never been dull on the pitch – with the Eagles either gunning for promotion or battling against relegation – it's been just as entertaining off it.

Observations on football and life from the colourful characters that have come through the doors of Selhurst Park have constantly kept us amused.

There's been Neil Warnock's hilarious tirades at referees, Ian Holloway's comic wisdom, Simon Jordan's rants at almost everybody and the strange musings from the eccentric Finn Aki Riihilahti.

Clinton Morrison was often prone to putting his foot in his mouth and remember some of Alan Smith's humorous sound bites? How about the barmy remarks from Steve Coppell or the brash statements from the larger-than-life Malcolm Allison?

Many of the crazy one-liners can be found here in this unique collection of quips and quotes and I hope you laugh as much reading this book as I did in compiling it.

Once you have finished, go to this address: www.holmesdale.net/madbonus where you will find some bonus quotes that I couldn't fit in these pages. I'd love to know the quotations that you liked best, so drop me a line at editor@holmesdale.net. Enjoy!

Gordon Law

"If we can get a result at Blackburn I'll give Alan a kiss."

Simon Jordan ahead of Alan Smith's first game back at the club

"The fans should bring their boots, especially if they can play at the back. And my hip's feeling a bit better, so we'll see."

Neil Warnock

"It's like Alan Partridge living out of a suitcase."

Scott Flinders on his latest club Hartlepool – the fifth side he had been loaned to

"I did not want Alan [Smith] to resign. I would have preferred to see Ron Noades squirm."

Gareth Southgate

"We now face three away games in seven days. If we win those games in the 1,200 miles we have to travel I'll bare my bum on the town hall steps."

Neil Warnock

"I didn't get on with Steve. We didn't connect. I don't click with people who are dour and, to a certain extent, disrespectful. He couldn't even be bothered to turn up to meetings."

Simon Jordan on Steve Coppell

"John Bond has blackened my name with his insinuations about the private lives of football managers. Both my wives are upset."

Malcolm Allison on his successor at Manchester City

"I've told them to go out, get drunk and take their phones off the hook."

Steve Coppell

"I'm not jumping on the Andy Johnson for England bandwagon – I'm driving it!

Iain Dowie

"We were negative, we played without passion, we were lacking in enthusiasm, we looked frightened and quite simply, we bottled it... At the end of the day players wearing our shirts didn't want the ball, didn't pass the ball, and I will even go to the extent of saying that they went hiding."

Dave Bassett

"I've just introduced Nigel Martyn to a clean sheet. The last time he had one Kenneth Wolstenholme was the commentator."

Steve Coppell

"It's up to the chairman to give me a present, but if it's down to him I'll get a big bunch of flowers. Dougie Freedman got a silver salver last season when he did it, so I'd like a gold one at least."

Clinton Morrison on reaching 100 Palace goals

"A lot of people thought Simon [Jordan] and I would fall out within weeks. One of us is outspoken, demanding and doesn't suffer fools gladly, and the other is, well, just the same."

Neil Warnock

"At the end of the day, it's all about what's on the shelf at the end of the year."
Steve Coppell

"It's like one of those fairy tales where you see a beautiful castle but when you get inside you discover years of decay. The princess, which is the players, is asleep. I'm trying to wake her but it takes more than one kiss."

Alan Smith

"Ashley-Paul is goin fulham on Monday. If I pull dis off I'm on dis ting!!!"

Palace Academy midfielder Ashley-Paul Robinson announces on Facebook he has a trial at Fulham. It backfires because he never plays for the Eagles again and ends up in non-league football

"You'd like to take him home with you and sit him in the living room cos he's such a nice kid. He's got a lovely sun tan but he wouldn't be big headed."

Alan Mullery on Vince Hilaire

"I should have been throwing rice instead of getting elbowed by a Rotherham defender. I feel really bad about missing my brother's wedding, a good party and a creamy strawberry cake."

Aki Riihilahti

"They are overpaid, under-achieving whingers."

Alan Smith

"The officials were the worst team tonight. They were indecisive throughout and there was practically manslaughter on James Scowcroft."

Neil Warnock

"He is basically a failed First Division footballer – if he is a good player he will prove his point with Swindon and throw the ball back in my face in a few years' time."

Steve Coppell on Paul Bodin

"I wouldn't be human if I didn't like pretty ladies. Once you stop looking, you're dead."

Malcolm Allison

"No doubt the ref will have gone down the pub, boasted to his mates that he sent off Neil Ruddock and felt proud of himself."

Neil Ruddock

"Unless I'm looking at Ronaldo or Messi, I'd never look at someone else and think he's better than me."

Wilfried Zaha

"No football-club owner in his right mind would willingly invite an average agent into his academy, any more than a brothel owner would let a syphilitic nutter into his brothel."

Simon Jordan

"I just yelled, 'Off you go, Cantona – it's an early shower for you!'"

Matthew Simmons, the Palace fan explaining what he said to Eric Cantona before the player 'kung-fo' assaulted him

"We need to tweak the nose of fear and stick an ice cube down the vest of terror."

Ian Holloway

"Sometimes I feel fit, sometimes I just feel the need to buy new hamstrings. I don't get any help from the weather, running in the heat makes it harder and me more red."

Aki Riihilahti

"It's nice to have two rather than one. As they say, you get one Chinese player and ten minutes later you want to buy another one."
Terry Venables on signing Fan Zhiyi and Sun Jihai

"Their goals were just comedy. You'd probably win £250 on Candid Camera for that second one."
Neil Warnock

"He's a big Palace fan and so is his mum and I think that if I hadn't got him she would have gone bananas."
Iain Dowie on Clinton Morrison

"I've had this number for 15 years and I'm not changing it for some daft bint."

Simon Jordan on getting a new mobile number due to Tara Stout harassing him

"I wouldn't take the England job for a big gold clock."

Steve Coppell

"If someone hates me when I've had a bad time they should trust me that no one hates me more than I do myself."

Shefki Kuqi

"As a father I've been tough at times – I took my son's four things he loved in his bedroom once. He had to behave himself to get them back, one a month. He was 13 and was misbehaving in class at school and wasn't fulfilling his ability. My dad wouldn't have put up with that. I think it was his music centre, television, games console and a Nintendo Game Boy. How harsh am I? But how bad was that for me at 50 years old? To be detached at Man United – did I deserve it? My wife will tell you I did."

Ian Holloway on having to watch Palace from the stands at Old Trafford after being banned from the dugout

"As a manager you're like a prostitute – you depend on other people for your living."
Steve Coppell after defeat to Hartlepool in the cup

"I'd like to lock up the guy at the tribunal who decided John Bostock should be sold to Tottenham for a packet of crisps."
Simon Jordan

Q: What sporting event would you pay most to watch?
A: Someone absolutely mashing Prince Nazeem Hamed.
David Hopkin in The Sun

"I think our players live in cloud cuckoo land. In training my best two are my coaches Glenn Cockerill and Ray Houghton. The bottom line is 'have we got any balls?' And the answer is 'no we haven't'."

Alan Smith

"We showed great bouncebackability."

Iain Dowie – the manager began using 'bouncebackability' during his press conferences in 2004 and the word was added to the Oxford English Dictionary on June 15, 2006.

"I accept the sack because of recent results but I find the manner of my dismissal unacceptable. When the boss Alan Smith spoke to me it was as if a total stranger was talking. Yet I worked with him for two years at Fulham and thought I had built up a friendship."

First-team coach Glenn Cockerill

"It's been very difficult working with him [administrator Brendan Guilfoyle], he has a high opinion of himself. I found out that the agent he brought in received £100,000 within days of selling Victor Moses for £2m and I think I could have sold him in my sleep."

Neil Warnock

"I needed a kick up the backside, I was getting too big for my boots."
Clinton Morrison

Photo: Gordon Law

"Hopefully this win will instil some confidence in the younger players, and until my nice boys turn into not so nice boys, then they won't get the edge they need."

Alan Smith

"Bill Wyman came to a match last year and I asked him if he still followed the results. He said, 'What do you mean, still f*cking follow the results? When you lose, I can't sleep for a f*cking week'."

Steve Parish

"I've got four lovely horses and I would have a terrible problem eating horsemeat."

Ian Holloway

"To be honest I thought in extra time both teams had settled for a replay. I was panicking then, because I hadn't re-booked our hotel for midweek."

Steve Coppell

"I read Simon Jordan's book and that's a load of rubbish."

Ron Noades

"I think the players looked like they would have rather been at home watching the Ryder Cup."
Trevor Francis

"I started to remember my younger years. I sure have some fine memories, because I actually scored once in training back in 1992!"
Aki Riihilahti, 2001

"We were woeful, out-fought, out-played, out-run, out-everything. We deserved nothing and we got nothing."
Manager Steve Kember after a 5-0 thrashing by Wigan Athletic

"On his first day at Palace he told me he wanted to play for England, a bold statement for someone who had just walked in off a building site."

Steve Coppell on Ian Wright

"I think the only chance we have of getting a penalty at the moment is somebody picking the ball up and throwing it at the referee. I said to the fourth official, 'How does it feel when you see you've made a mistake.' He said, 'It hurts.' So there will be one or two people hurting tonight."

Neil Warnock

"I could be political and say it's football and these things happen, which is true. But, to be completely honest, I felt like someone had kicked me right in the testicles."
Julian Speroni on manager Dougie Freedman quitting

Photo: Keith Gillard

"I couldn't stay [at Palace]. They were run by a bunch of liars."

Sasa Curcic

"My mother-in-law had intended to do the hoovering that afternoon while she watched [the 1990 A Cup semi-final]. She never started. She just stood and watched the whole game leaning on the bloody hoover."

Gary O'Reilly

"They said I lost the changing room. I know where it is, it's down the corridor on the left."

Ian Holloway

"I always thought Palace were a bit flighty, a bit flash, lacking in substance – a legacy of Terry Venables and Malcolm Allison. In human form we were the Fast Show character – a little bit tasty, a little bit 'whoooar', a little bit 'wayyy'.
Simon Jordan

"My friends are getting married and having children. That is lovely. I instead am only married with a round object. Football is not an especially good wife. At the moment I am closer to having a rock concert at Wembley than getting married. I am not a good singer."
Aki Riihilahti

"I have been there for 12 months and he has spoken about two words in the time I have known him."

Trevor Francis on Alex Kolinko

"People say that me and Ian [Holloway] are very similar. Other than Ian being a lot uglier than me, we're both passionate, we both care about our teams and we've both done it the hard way."

Neil Warnock

"Their goal was against the run of play and Stuart Taylor had nothing to do in goal. In fact, my mum could have played there."

Alan Smith

"I'll keep signing him till he's nearly 50 or 60 if he keeps putting the ball in the net."

Ian Holloway on Kevin Phillips

"Yes, we do get women after us in this game. But I'm old fashioned. I like to do the chasing – at least, I used to before I married."

Malcolm Allison

"On many occasions I wondered what on earth I was doing when we lost and, when we'd lost, I readily admit that I would have been happier going to prison than driving into the training ground."

Steve Coppell on early days of being a manager

"At the end of the day, I have a certain hairstyle. Whether I'm too old to carry it off now, I'm not sure. But it's a subject for discussion, and there's only one thing worse than people talking about you – and that's people not talking about you."

Simon Jordan

"His house burnt down and all his gear got burnt and I think that did him a favour!"
Ben Watson on Leon Cort

Photo: Peter Guntrip

"If they want me to explain my comments, I'm not going to. They're there to read in the paper... They need to spend their time tackling the problems the column identified instead of bothering me."

Simon Jordan on being charged by the FA over his newspaper article about referees

"When you come back into the job, you want to do everything right, you want to be articulate and you don't want to start criticising referees. Then you start becoming as big a lunatic as everybody else."

Alan Smith

MAD ALL OVER

"I think the players really need to look at themselves. I had all 16 of them in the dressing room for one-and-a-half hours and only four of them had anything to say and two of them are on loan, that says it all. Someone said that they were giving their all but if that is their best I'd hate to see what their worst is. Instead of worrying what car they're driving they need to concentrate on the game. We were beaten by good honest professional players. I took them to an Italian restaurant last Thursday, paid for it myself and it was quite nice. They didn't like the lasagne, though, they wanted spaghetti bolognese! If these attitudes don't change, it will be anarchy and you'll have the lunatics running the asylum. I feel like Michael Caine in Zulu. A pistol in my hand, 16,000 coming over the hill trying to claim my head. I can't shoot all of them so I might as well shoot the three fellas nearest me who are causing all of the problems."

Alan Smith

"The ones that booed me, and I have to say it wasn't everyone, are the worst set of fans at a club I've been at."

Shefki Kuqi on the Palace supporters

"I was asked how I'd handle a player doing what Craig Bellamy did to Newcastle and I said what I felt: I'd strangle him with his own tongue."

Simon Jordan

"If we say, 'You have the ball and have a go, then we'll have the ball and have a go.' Then we're going to get beaten. Heavily."

Steve Coppell

"I need to go shopping most weeks. I run out of milk, I run out of eggs, I run out of bread, I need to get a paper. But you can't do that, can you? If you're the Premier League team and the window's closed and you run out of centre forwards, and you ain't got any left, you can't go shopping until the window opens again. And then there's a mad rush in January. So all you lot wait until there's a mad rush and you start speculating on who's done any good in that window and before it closes you're all talking about them. The little bloke with his little machine – how boring is it? Let's turn over and see some real life. Why do you put speculation on things when it hasn't happened yet? If it happens, then great we'll tell you about it. But in the meantime, what about the rest of my team?"

Ian Holloway

"We've lost seven games 1-0 and drawn another seven 0-0. If we'd drawn the 1-0 games we lost, we'd have another seven points. If the seven draws had been 1-0 to us, we'd have 28 points more and we'd be third in the Premiership instead of going down."
Alan Smith

"If anyone can understand Alex they're doing well. The problem is he's a committed 15st bloke, who comes for everything, but doesn't call!"
Dean Austin on Alex Kolinko

"Millwall getting a beating at home!??"
Nathaniel Clyne

Photo: Magnus Andersson

"Nobody's about so I have been doing things I never even thought I would be doing like pricing up grass seed."

Dougie Freedman on life at the training ground after Paul Hart left

"We had our Christmas party at Crystal Palace during the week – and I am happy to report that my directors didn't ask me to copy Blackburn boss Henning Berg by dressing up to do a song and dance routine."

Ian Holloway

"Leon [Cort] was a reluctant sale but we're a very nice team and the Championship is a tough league."

Neil Warnock

"As soon as the new manager [Warnock] came in he was saying things like I didn't have enough scars on my face and I knew my time was up."

Leon Cort

"A lot of people don't expect me to be any use to Palace. Then a lot of people talk sh*t."

Tomas Brolin

"When I scored I said, 'Thank you John, thank you'. He was very happy. He was crying and kissing me. Everyone was jumping on me. Then I said to John, 'Ow!', I think my ribs are broken!'"

Nicola Ventola hails fitness coach John Harbin after his goal against Southampton

"[Simon] Jordan has had plenty of opportunity to ask me for help. He could have always rung me up. But he's been too pig-headed to do that or big-headed."

Ron Noades

"If we get a little bit complacent we know we're going to get our bottoms spanked so we have to keep things in perspective."

Neil Warnock

"My job is to be invisible, work hard and do it simple for the team. Just like I am with girls: even though I work hard they treat me as invisible and simple."

Aki Riihilahti

"Even if I built a 50,000 seat stadium and bought Ronaldinho, there'd still be complaints about crap hot dogs."

Simon Jordan

"The result of all this moist-eyed, village-idiot sentimentality is men like Brian Curson, our referee at Reading in midweek. No doubt he's a human, emotional, decent man. But is he someone who should be in charge of top-level football games?"

Simon Jordan

"Attilio Lombardo is starting to pick up a bit of English on the training ground. The first word he learned was 'w*nker'."

Steve Coppell

"I was not asking for the moon."

Attilio Lombardo on his wage demands

"One young [Bristol City] yobbo caught me. I think one of the security guards trod on him as he fell to the floor because I heard him squeal. He needs his eyesight looking at because he was that close I don't know how he missed, he just grazed me. There's millions of people who would like to do that!"

Neil Warnock

"He dived. He should be embarrassed. He's a great professional and that's unlike him. I haven't spoken to him about it but I don't need to. He will see the replay and he will be embarrassed."

Alan Pardew on James McArthur

"I haven't sworn for almost a week now. When I saw a film of my sortie into the centre circle at the final whistle, I could quite clearly see myself mouth a number of obscenities at the referee. And I was ashamed of myself. That was why I accepted the FA's charge of improper conduct and paid a £2,000 fine. In fact, my behaviour cost me a grand total of £2,012 – because I also had to pay a £12 'fine' to my wife Kim after initially telling her that I hadn't sworn."

Ian Holloway

"I was performing a character from the Dumb & Dumber movie in the locker room. Next day the doctor diagnosed that I had concussion and some nasty bumps (I hope he did not mean my nose)."

Aki Riihilahti

"He wet his knickers about buying the place."

Ron Noades on Mark Goldberg

"I have no problem with Ben [Watson]. One or two of his acquaintances I have a problem with."

Neil Warnock

"I've realised I'm hideously ugly when I don't get what I want. My dad said to me years ago, 'What's the point in arguing?' I wish I was more like Bjorn Borg – but I'm probably more like John McEnroe in temperament, but not in skill."

Ian Holloway

"I was a left-winger and signed schoolboy forms with Chelsea. The truth is I was quite arrogant, if I didn't get the ball where I wanted it on the pitch I would stand there shouting, 'I wanted it f*cking here, not there!'."

Simon Jordan

"Me and Clinton are working very well, we understand each other on the pitch. I don't really understand him off the pitch, what he says."
Dougie Freedman

"To win anything in life you have to go to places like Cardiff."
Alan Smith

"If that was a penalty then there are six or seven a match."
Steve Coppell on Hartlepool's spot-kick following an apparent push in the area

"I am disgusted. If I had known this rule, I would have a clause in my contract. But my advisor did not tell me. And now I am told that it is almost my fault. It is true, I have a proper contract, I earn a little more than Bordeaux but living in London is 10 times more expensive. And I came to play. Either I rip up my contract or I wait until the winter transfer window to find a club."

New signing Florian Marange after failing to make Palace's 25-man squad

"We lost [at Bristol City] but I was not at fault for the two goals. I have only had seven or eight training sessions. How can you judge a player after 10 days? I have never been presented to the press, I have never had an official photo and I am still waiting for my club suit. I stayed for 15 days in a hotel before finding somewhere to live and the club told me I had to pick up the bill."

Florian Marange

"It's a hard place to come for a southern team. You can dress well and have all the nice watches in the world but that won't buy us a result at Grimsby."

Alan Smith

"He is not just here to take the cream."

Steve Coppell on Attilio Lombardo

"[Shefki] Kuqi missed a good chance, it went to his head. He could have just controlled it, but that's Kuqi for you."

Neil Warnock

"The chairman has said that I should have asked permission to go on holiday. How petty is that? In 14 years as a professional I've never asked permission to go on holiday! I'm not happy."

Dean Austin

"After that we got some drive. We got them and were just about to pass them. We were in the faster line with the faster car. Then the invisible truck forced us to pull over."

Aki Riihilahti

"Being manager of this club is like wheeling a trolley round Sainsbury's. You want it to go one way, the trolley wants to go the other."

Alan Smith

"I would like to keep my money in my pocket and pay for my other daughter's wedding next summer. Come to the pub and I will tell you exactly what I feel. I can't make anything of it because my opinion doesn't count. I've realised that now."

Ian Holloway

"In my first season when I was absolutely appalled at the players' performance. I stormed in and said, 'Here's a newsflash for you f*ckers. If you think you're going to undermine me or the manager you are wrong. Each and every one of you will go before me. If you don't want to pull your fingers out, form an orderly queue outside my office on Monday morning and you can all f*ck off.' We won the next 11 games, but then we went down the toilet and nearly got relegated."

Simon Jordan

"I believe we can fight for promotion. If I did not believe that, I might just instead travel back to Finland and open a Turkish kebab restaurant. I did not come to England to do something I don't believe in. I want to win. That is why I don't like kebabs."

Aki Riihilahti

"I made the players spar with these gloves for the last few days. I did it because I knew our match against Watford would be a fight."

Alan Smith

"When we were signing players like Neil Ruddock, Harry Redknapp had told me we had to get him on a weight clause in his contract otherwise he would turn up overweight. It's one thing me saying, 'Listen, you're f*cking fat, lose weight or we're going to put you on a weight contract', and it is another thing if a manager says it, but Steve [Coppell] wouldn't."

Simon Jordan

"Charlton is the only place I can go and not be the number one most hated man if the chairman [Simon Jordan] turns up. I hope he is going."

Neil Warnock

"Sometimes it can be difficult when you have played one position all year and then you are asked to play somewhere else. It can become confusing."

Hayden Mullins

"I'm stunned. Only last week I was offered a new contract and I thought I was doing a good job. Then, bang you're out."

Reserve team boss Dave Swindlehurst

"I think [Andy] Dawson is a fine young prospect with a big future ahead of him but I would rather have seen him in the bath."

Trevor Francis

"There were plenty of fireworks on the pitch, but the only flares on display were those on Nigel's suit."

Iain Dowie on Nigel Worthington

"Aki Riihilahti, a ridiculous person in the best possible way – committed, brilliant work ethic, bit bonkers and totally engaging."

Simon Jordan

"I don't think Neil [Warnock] should complain about referees. I've told him that. I don't think it helps us with matches."

Steve Parish

"I'm not nice when I don't get what I want. But my mum would have washed my mouth if she had seen what the officials wrote down from what I said to them after Spurs. I've eaten a bar of soap before and then I swear like a trooper!"
Ian Holloway

"[David] Elleray went around with his arms folded like a school teacher. Which, of course, he is."
Simon Jordan

"Fortunately, Graham Poll's retired so I won't have a problem from that point of view – there'll be no blame placed on him this time."

Neil Warnock

"How bad it is to spend a New Year's Eve in the hotel (bed time at 10pm), concentrate and be fired up for a game that is called off next day. Especially when apparently Russian ballet girls were staying at the same hotel."

Aki Riihilahti

"This was a valuable three points. It's now a question of keeping your marbles."

Alan Smith

"I bumped in to Robbie [Savage] and he told me he'd had fans singing, 'There's only one Simon Jordan' to him. Look, I live in Spain, I'm not going to sit in the shade, so I'll get a tan, and my hair is short now, so it's a redundant question."

Simon Jordan

"I don't think he's spoken since he signed."

Ben Watson on Leon Cort

"I found that fella who can control me – and that's me."

Malcolm Allison

"I was very disappointed by their goal and when I turned round I saw Kolinko laughing so I cuffed him around the ear. It was only a bit of fun and the view was actually better from the stand."

Trevor Francis after the draw with Bradford City

"I was not laughing in the dugout. The manager punched me on the nose. I have not been given an explanation why he did it. My nose is very sore and bruised."

Alex Kolinko

"My players say I look like Pete Burns but I don't know who he is. All I know is he's obviously not blessed with good looks."

Iain Dowie

"After the financial problems the club has been in previously, many people seem to think they can kick us in the nuts."

Steve Parish

"Julian Speroni has been super, the challenge on him was a bit naughty. But if he was my player I would have told him to have gone in like that, I don't like goalkeepers!"

Neil Warnock

"The best thing about Christmas is the day it's over. I'm not a big Christmas fan. I don't usually eat Christmas dinner and I don't really celebrate it. I don't do presents, I'm not interested any more."
Damien Delaney

"As I was going past the Scarborough dressing room, all their players were in the bath and I could hear them saying, 'What do you think about that big-headed b*stard? First chance we ever have of getting some publicity and he comes along in that stupid hat'."

Malcolm Allison

"Players get their wages for working seven days a week, not just for 45 minutes in the second half."

Alan Smith

"It's very rare I get down. You can put too much emphasis on the wrong things. I've a great friend I talk to who is a farmer. Some of the things he has to do, something breaks and he fixes them. It's just amazing."

Ian Holloway

"There is no doubt he is a charmer, but when you look at his record it isn't that great. He didn't need to qualify for Euro 96 and his only major English trophy is an FA Cup. Goldberg wanted Venables to lift morale, but that cost him £1m a year."

Simon Jordan on Terry Venables

MAD ALL OVER

"I made up a story about Alex Kolinko, who had been in tears after the game. I said he came from the poorest mountain village in Latvia where he had to fight bears when he was eight. I said his grandparents had been shot by the Nazis, his mother had died of cancer and his sister was raped by a gang of mountain rebels. But he never shed a single tear because he was strong and brave. Then I told them that one month playing behind our defence had turned him into a blubbering wreck! The players didn't know what to say. Except Clinton Morrison – he said, 'It's a shame about his sister'."

Alan Smith

"We will have to be slightly different away from home, but part of our game is drawing teams onto us and then knocking them out with a [sucker] punch. I don't think we are going to be a Sugar Ray Leonard, I think we are going to be more of a Muhammad Ali against Joe Frasier."

Ian Holloway

"The league table looks now in our eyes more like that minging woman bus driver from South Park than sweet Shakira. Even the table lamp is gone. It was accidentally executed in a moment of anger after the Watford game."

Aki Riihilahti

"I did say I wouldn't sell it [the ground] to him on one occasion because he stood on stage at Fairfield Hall and said that I'd be dead by the time the lease ran out which I didn't think was very nice."

Ron Noades on Simon Jordan

"After all the disappointments and frustration I look the league table now and there is again this same enthusiastic feeling like in the younger years in the candy stores. We can still get our candy. Which is otherwise good – except for the English dental care system."

Aki Riihilahti

"I was up like a little kid at 6.30am. I couldn't sleep thinking about the fixtures. So I just got up to watch Sky Sports until they came out!"
Peter Ramage

"I knew I could play before, but in the First Division I learnt how to wrestle. It toughened me up so now, I can play and wrestle. I say a big 'thank you' to Palace."

Mikael Forssell

"We've tried to sign several players but other clubs have come in. It's a bit like the girl that you fancy is attracted to someone else, so you've got to be crafty and hit the dance floor before everyone else."

Alan Smith

"We will need everyone at Selhurst Park pulling in the right direction and not just the players. We need the directors, the kit man, the programme sellers and the tea lady all in it together."

Ian Holloway

"I'm not going to drag it out or make a point, because points are pointless."

Simon Jordan

"I wanted to make sure that we kept an eye on the offsides so I had my subs warming up with the linesman."

Neil Warnock

"I brought my son tonight because he wanted to see [Emmanuel] Adebayor – I told him he wouldn't get a kick and I was right!"

Neil Warnock after the Carling Cup loss to Manchester City

"I am going to have a look at the video, but if that is an eight-booking game and two sendings-off, then I am a Dutchman."

Iain Dowie

"Neil Warnock has been an inspiration to me. But sometimes on the line me and him do clash a little bit."

Ian Holloway

"I would like to inform that I'm missing three pounds of fat, one hamstring muscle and a ridiculous amount of sweat somewhere in the Beckenham area. If found, please contact the knackered looking blond geezer or at least buy the poor fellow a Lucozade."

Aki Riihilahti

"It didn't take an Einstein to work out that this match was never going to take place. The officials could have phoned Michael Fish. He would have told them not to bother because it was going to rain all day."

Alan Smith

"I had a successful advertising business employing 3,000 people in 13 countries. But you know what? My school never asked me to come back and talk to the pupils... Then I bought a loss-making football club in South London and suddenly everyone wants to talk to me and hear my views on the world!"

Steve Parish

"I told him to calm down a bit. To be fair he didn't do much – he was concerned about his lad who had blood coming out of his nose. If he wants me to speak for him I will do – I know everyone on the commission!"

Neil Warnock after QPR manager Paulo Sousa was sent to the stand

"Sometimes when you cool down at half-time you become very stiff."
Iain Dowie

"I threw those poor old ripped and stinky things [shin pads] into the stands. Later I heard a couple of supporters had fainted because of the smell. They evacuated this stand and it is still classed as chemical danger area."

Aki Riihilahti

"It's quite interesting that my most disciplined players happen to be two Latvians, one Finnish guy and a Chinese guy."

Alan Smith

"I believe I could sell a fridge to an Eskimo."

Ian Holloway

"I'm not looking to lose fans, and as much as I appreciate their support, I just wish they'd count to 10 a bit more."

Peter Taylor

"I had an Aston Martin phone worth £15,000 given to me as a present. I dropped it in a gin and tonic about 15 seconds after opening it."

Simon Jordan

"We were doing great before they scored five freak goals."

Bert Head

"What does Everton chairman Bill Kenwright think he will get for £6m? Andy Johnson's trainers."

Simon Jordan

"If you score, you often just bellow like a horny animal and do these ridiculous madman celebrations that would in normal life get you hospitalised. And when the ball goes a bit wide from the target, everybody raises their hands, throws their necks and sighs: 'Ooooh!' I can't really see a barber doing that just because he cut the customer's mullet a bit too short."

Aki Riihilahti

"It's a horrible process. I'll have millions of texts from Carlos Fandango and if he's not, they'll make a person up and give him to me. It's great that everybody wants the job. It's very difficult to sift that."

Steve Parish

"I think the new owners for City have been absolutely fantastic. We're trying to find one of these Sheikhs, wherever they are. We're hoping they come to the match and bring their family. Then hopefully a brother, a sister, an uncle or an auntie can take a fancy to us and put a bid in to Simon Jordan."

Neil Warnock

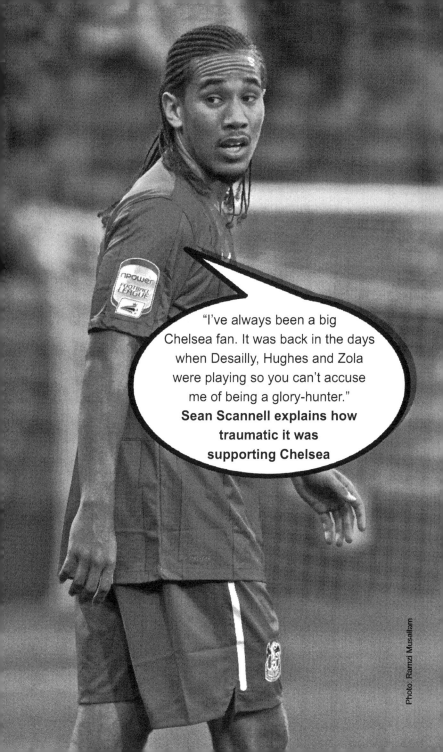

"I've always been a big Chelsea fan. It was back in the days when Desailly, Hughes and Zola were playing so you can't accuse me of being a glory-hunter."
Sean Scannell explains how traumatic it was supporting Chelsea

Photo: Ramzi Musallam

"I think that he plays for himself. I think he plays for the crowd. If he played for the team he wouldn't be running over to get himself sent off against Norwich."

Simon Jordan on Jamie Pollock

"I personally don't think he's a good player but I don't pick the team. If the new manager wants to pick Jamie Pollock, I will listen to what he has to say."

Simon Jordan on Jamie Pollock

"The first goal was a foul, the second was offside, and they would never have scored the third if they hadn't got the other two."

Steve Coppell on losing to Liverpool

"We are staying in a nice hotel, a country club. I have got a beautician coming in who will manicure their nails."

Alan Smith looking after his players

"If Andy [Johnson] doesn't like it he can throw his toys out of the pram, but will that really help his England chances? I don't think so."

Simon Jordan

"Charlton's players should be disgusted with themselves – if they'd put that effort in when [their manager] Alan Pardew was here they would not be in the position. They don't play Crystal Palace every week."

Neil Warnock

"You show me your performance when you throw your shirt down and it is three or four kilos in weight because you have run your socks off and spilled blood for the cause."

Ian Dowie

"My players need to run and make runs."

Ian Holloway

"Clinton loves to milk any situation and be the centre of attention. Let's face it, we are never going to take the Clinton out of Morrison. And since managers have tantrums then why shouldn't players be allowed to as well."

Alan Smith

"Let's hope me and the players can have a decent marriage."

Ian Holloway

"My Saturday night ends late on Sunday morning – it's devoted exclusively to birds and booze."

Mel Blyth

"I can't even stand the sight of seeing him after everything I've done for the kid. I've looked after him and his family ever since he signed for the club and then he treats me with utter contempt."

Simon Jordan on Julian Gray

"Things are pretty tight at the moment. I've cut out the starter on my lunch at the training ground – I'm down to the main course and the dessert now!"

Neil Warnock

"I'm from Brighton which won't please the Palace fans, the Millwall fans aren't that happy either and I have mates from Leeds who have been giving me stick as well. I'm getting it from all angles."
Paul Ifill

"Thanks to the crowd for the 'one Robbie Savage' chant. No, I'm not changing my haircut, it's dandy."
Simon Jordan

"The big monster called relegation is there, ready to bite us on the arse."
Steve Coppell

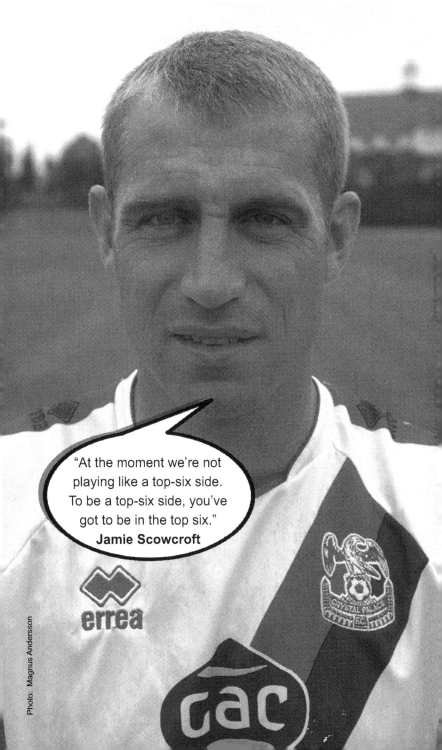

"At the moment we're not playing like a top-six side. To be a top-six side, you've got to be in the top six."
Jamie Scowcroft

"Injuries are like ketchup: first there is long quiet period but then suddenly there comes out a big wave of sh*t."

Aki Riihilahti

"He doesn't speak English and he's nervous off the pitch. But, when he starts to communicate better he'll be a good keeper."

Alan Smith on Alex Kolinko

"This really is squeaky-bum time, and we have all got to show that we've got the bottle to come through it."

Ian Holloway

"I wasn't surprised I recovered so quickly – it was a German doctor after all."

Marco Reich

"I certainly don't agree when he says he didn't move for the money. Money is a big thing for Shefki [Kuqi]."

Neil Warnock

"People miss penalties. People say not by that much, mind!"

Tony Pulis on Jason Puncheon's misdirected spot-kick against Spurs

"I'm no respecter of tradition and I have no time for the Manchester Uniteds and Arsenals of this world. There's nothing to admire in these clubs. They're just bullsh*t worlds full of bullsh*t people."
Simon Jordan

"What I like about is I love looking at him, he is such a happy man and he makes me feel good."
Neil Warnock on Alassane N'Diaye

"Promotion would be another notch in my football bedpost."
Ian Holloway

"In the wake of a bad penalty and people's opinions and banter which I accept. @mattletiss7 [Matt Le Tissier] on TalkSPORT this morning gets it right. Everything else is banter and opinions and as a man I will live with that, which is fine, but I will not live with his opinion."

Jason Puncheon hits out at pundit Neil Warnock who criticised his penalty miss against Tottenham

"[My mum] is happy. She only lives five minutes around the corner so she is buzzing."

Clinton Morrison

"Without Laurel and Hardy, Laurel wouldn't be Hardy."
Ian Holloway

Photo: Keith Gillard

"Somebody from a high authority told me that he had a bit of barney with the chairman. Hopefully, with whatever has happened between Iain Dowie and the chairman, it can be sorted."

Clinton Morrison

"Clinton needs to engage his brain before he opens his mouth, and he will be told that. He needs to learn when to speak and when to be quiet, and Clinton should not talk about people like Iain Dowie and myself. When he comes back from international duty, he will probably be given a kick up the backside."

Simon Jordan

"The goals we're giving away are unacceptable. I wouldn't expect to see them on a Sunday in a local park."

Mark Kennedy

"That pigeonhole is off our back."

Tony Pulis happy about the changing perceptions of his team's style of play

"If anyone is counting their chickens, they haven't hatched out yet. You can look at the eggs, but you don't know how many chickens you're going to get, so we'll just sit in there and have a go."

Ian Holloway

"He used to sell mobile phones and I suppose he has a different mentality."

Steve Coppell on Simon Jordan

"Our job is to try and do our best for Crystal Malice, I mean Palace."

Tomas Brolin

"When I was here as manager in 1994 there were two egos – me and the chairman – and there is only one who is going to win."

Alan Smith

"It was a bad miss and it gets worse every time you look at it. And instead of going a goal up we lose by three, which could have been five. I've told Neil [Danns] to come up and tell you how he missed it. I'm not sure he will though."

Neil Warnock

"It's about bedding this group in and making sure that they know how to speak to each other and what's acceptable. Anyone with more than one dog, when you introduce another one, you get a few problems."

Ian Holloway

"Dave Bassett has said he could not work with me and he is right. He is a dinosaur whose time has gone."

Simon Jordan

"I look forward to sharing some conversation after the match, but I'll let Sir Alex do the drinking."

Dougie Freedman

"I remember all [my opponents'] names, faces and situations, those b*stards."

Aki Riihilahti

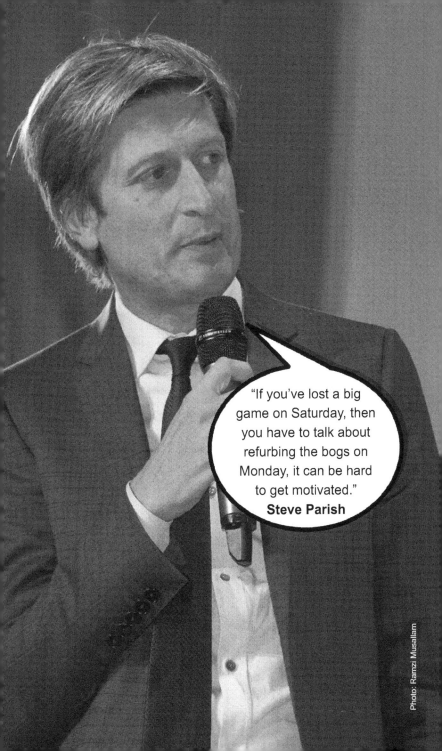

"If you've lost a big game on Saturday, then you have to talk about refurbing the bogs on Monday, it can be hard to get motivated."
Steve Parish

"It was a real disappointment to me because when she got in the bath I realised she had plastic tits. It wasn't worth getting the sack for." **Malcolm Allison reflects on his decision to invite glamour model Fiona Richmond to the training ground shortly before he was fired for bad results**

"[Pain is] someone non-stop kicking your genitals combined with a century's hangover while Sepultura is playing in the background. Sometimes it could be better to be unconscious."
Aki Riihilahti

"The gaffer wanted me to kiss him but if my missus had seen me kissing him I would have been in trouble!"

Clinton Morrison declines to snog Peter Taylor

"I wanted him to kiss me but he bottled it. I don't ask all my players to kiss me – just Clinton because I fancy him."

Taylor can't hide his disappointment

"I'd rather support Millwall than sell Andy Johnson."

Simon Jordan

"Ron Noades is the Fidel Castro of football, an enlightened despot rather than a dictator."
Steve Coppell

"It got to the stage where I said to him, 'I realise what you are now. You're not a coach, Malcolm, you're a professional luncher!'"
Coach Terry Venables on manager Malcolm Allison preferring to meet for lunch instead of taking training

"It was like I used to say when I was a manager up north, we looked like southern softies."
Neil Warnock

"Without being arrogant, I am probably the highest-profile club chairman in the country. Whether it is because I am young or I fight causes or I have a big mouth or I date silly girls, I don't know."

Simon Jordan

"He's the loudest player you have ever heard in your life. You'd be able to hear him from a mile away. He's non-stop. If he's not talking he's moaning. About everything."

Ben Watson on Clinton Morrison

"You could see I've got a lot of control over him cos I called him over and told him to calm down and then he nearly got booked twice in the next two minutes."

Neil Warnock on Marouane Chamakh

"I did consider [becoming a ball-winning midfielder], but when I went in for tackles I started crying afterwards."

Tom Ince

"We shall have to get the armour out and polish it up for the replay."

Arthur Wait

"I'm not some stupid 19-year-old 'greenhorn' and I won't allow them to play games with me."
Gabor Kiraly unhappy with his initial terms

"So what does the future bring for Ian Holloway? Well, I've only been out of football for a few days, but I already feel like a man who has been stranded on a desert island. As the character played by Tom Hanks in the film Castaway said, 'I'll just wait to see what the tide brings in'."

Ian Holloway

"Agents are scum. They're evil, divisive and pointless. They only survive because the rest of the sport is so corrupt and because leading football club people employ their sons in the job."

Simon Jordan

"He was giving it the old big-time Charlie. He can't help being a prat. He didn't want to shake hands. They were under orders. They kept slowing the game down by throwing balls onto the pitch. It certainly leaves a bit of a bad taste. And Warnock wonders why people don't like him?"

Steve Kember refused to shake hands with Neil Warnock after defeat to Sheffield United

"In some ways I admire football fans because in what other business can you serve up crap and then have people come back for more?"

Simon Jordan

"He can be very sarcastic. As a foreigner, it was sometimes difficult to understand when he was being serious or if he was joking."

Aki Riihilahti on Alan Smith

"It's almost an assault. He [Craig Dawson] comes from two or three yards away and smashes him [Julian Speroni] in the face. I don't understand why at least one of the officials can't see that. I have not seen something like that since Bert Trautmann."

Neil Warnock

"I don't give a f*ck about football protocol and the other club owners. They want me to sit and have lunch before the games. F*ck that. I don't go to football to drink Chardonnay in the boardrooms with those tossers. I go to win games. I don't have anything in common with 90 per cent of football club chairmen. They don't interest me."

Simon Jordan

"He's been openly critical of the players, saying we're not mentally strong enough. Ultimately Alan [Smith] picks the team, chooses the tactics and buys the players with the money at his disposal."

Dean Austin

"He doesn't know what he's going to do next, so the full-back doesn't have a chance, does he?"

Neil Warnock on Yannick Bolasie

"The referee had a real stinker. At one stage I thought he was going to book the corner flag."

Arthur Wait

"Moving to Manchester will be something I have to get used too... I will come down to see my family so I do not think my accent will change!"

Wilfried Zaha

"He's our player. I paid for him and he will have to be prised from my dead hand before he leaves here."

Simon Jordan on Andy Johnson

"Neil Warnock keeps on getting Kieran Djilali and myself mixed up because we have the same first name – so my first task is to make sure he knows who I am."

Kieron Cadogan

"I'm the man who steers the ship and we've run aground. I can't blame the rudder."

Steve Coppell

"Some [chairmen] want to have stature within the community. Others, like David Dein, want to live vicariously through their clubs, their deeds being magnified by the deeds of others."

Simon Jordan

"I love David Dein for his total Arsenalness. He's one of those people who'll always come up to you, shake your hand, ask how things are going and then stiff you in the nicest possible way."

Simon Jordan

"I was summoned by the chairman-to-be and was proposed the [manager's] job there and then. I had half-an-hour to make a decision, and it felt like being run over by a lorry."

Attilio Lombardo

"South London is ours, South London is ourssss. F*ck off Millwall, South London is ours. Lol, feeling #Gladallover."

Nathaniel Clyne

"I'm very disappointed and I will apologise to my chairman when I phone him up later."

Peter Taylor on the cup defeat to Notts County

"There's no place for a chairman in the dressing room. Simon Jordan is verbally very, very aggressive and it rubs people up the wrong way. I found it oppressive and had to leave."

Steve Coppell

"When I didn't play, my coach Peter Taylor told me he's happy that I wasn't resentful and helped my goalkeeper teammate. He wished everyone would be as professional as I am. Now am I a real professional, or an unwanted person? Our manager is very unpredictable as a human and as a coach, too."

Gabor Kiraly

"I may be the cheapest, but I can still get the most expensive players with my hardest tackles."

Aki Riihilahti not fussed by his low transfer value in fantasy football

"I think experienced referees should stay on but if Clive's [Penton] not fit enough to keep up with play there, that's not on."

Neil Warnock

"He was a shocking waste of money."

Simon Jordan on Andrejs Rubins

"Why do the media relish slagging off Selhurst Park so much? There's one big reason: the media facilities aren't that great. And why's that? Because the media have consistently had a go at me for the last five years, so I took their biscuits away."

Simon Jordan

"As the manager I have to believe we can beat relegation. I'm in Miracle on 34th Street. If you've seen the film, that's me. I believe in Father Christmas."

Iain Dowie

"We couldn't pass water!"
Neil Warnock

Photo: Magnus Andersson

errea

GAC Logistics

"I am totally stunned and disgusted at the way this has been handled. This is just typical of the incompetents who run the Football League. They should simply be sacked."

Simon Jordan on the failed ITV Digital broadcast deal which put many clubs into financial trouble

"We have come out of a nuclear war with these people, there are bodies everywhere, and they are still dictating to us."

Simon Jordan on a new ITV contract agreed with clubs shortly afterwards

"I don't think I'll comment further – last season it cost me a £2,000 fine from the FA. Then again, shall I read you what Carlos Queiroz said about one ref when he was with Man United? [Pulling out a piece of paper from his pocket]. He called the ref a 'disgrace' but he didn't get fined, did he?"

Neil Warnock

"To be fair, the Premiership is a jungle and we are starting to rumble. We have players people have never heard of, but we're proud of the performances."

Aki Riihilahti

"In training, our objective has been to reduce the opposition's scoring opportunities whilst increasing our own."

Malcolm Allison's plan to win football matches

"I did enough algebra when I was at university, so I am sick and tired of that."

Iain Dowie on working out how many points needed to survive

"Eric Young was a cold, blunt b*stard but not a bad bloke."

Andy Woodman

"I was upset at the end, definitely. For a start, I couldn't understand why the fourth official was busy shaking hands with the Birmingham bench while we were trying to send on our third substitute Johannes Ertl. I would have thought that was more important."

Neil Warnock

"My name is so long that they told me they are running out of the letter 'I', and could I wear 'Aki' on my back instead! I think it's because of all the replica shirts I've been buying for my friends and family."

Aki Riihilahti

"At the minute, the dish we're making tastes lovely, like one of those puddings on MasterChef. It won't take much for it to burn or go soggy, but their focus is awesome. They are getting it just right."

Ian Holloway

"Scowie is the most boring man I have ever met – he's got the worst gear I have ever seen and he's the hairiest man I have ever seen. There's not a lot going for him, it's a good job he can play football!"

Ben Watson on James Scowcroft

"He keeps scoring against me the sod!"
Peter Taylor on Burnley's Ade Akinbiyi

"There were too many people – the whole 11 in fact – who for whatever reason were doing their own thing. At least I am paid to watch it unlike the fans who came here. I am sure they will go home absolutely disgusted. Even if Tom Finney had played at his age he would have had a good game against us."

Alan Smith

"It was a great social life under Malcolm [Allison]. But the football was crap."

Alan Whittle

"It's a labour of love with 'labour' being the operative word. It's at best unrewarding, at worst demoralising. And f*cking easy to get into, but bloody hard to get out."

Simon Jordan on running Palace

"They have such a strong crowd and that can work against them. It makes them go forward and forward and you can hit back and catch them with their trousers down."

Terry Venables on Sunderland

"I tried to get a pen and write a 'For Sale' sign on him but he was too quick for me."

Neil Warnock on Shefki Kuqi

"It was nice to get some monetary reward from the Brighton fans."
Iain Dowie on being hit by coins after Palace's late winner

"In terms of the credibility the papers have in dressing rooms, I've had players arguing their worth based on the marks out of 10 they get in The Sun."
Simon Jordan

"[Curtis Fleming] is teaching me how to speak a bit of Irish and drink Guinness. I'm struggling. I only really know how to drink Guinness."
Clinton Morrison

"He told me he wants to be in Europe within 18 months. Whether that means we're all going to Majorca next summer, I don't know."

Neil Warnock on Simon Jordan's lofty ambitions

"My wife nearly left me for the first time in the 38 years we've been together."

Tony Pulis says transfer talks with Steve Parish was putting a strain on his marriage

"As long as you hit the target they go in, if the keeper don't make a save."

Ian Holloway

"I wouldn't be certain
of winning if we were
five goals up with a
few minutes to go."
Alan Smith

Photo: Andy Roberts

"I was called every name under the sun by hundreds of morons outside the [Bristol City] ground. They called me a poof, they called me orange and plenty of other insults that you could not print. They were being particularly vitriolic, but I just kept my head down. What can you do? They are morons."

Simon Jordan

"Did we know we were going to spend that much? No. The chairman was like a kid in a sweet shop."

Ian Holloway on Steve Parish

"I was playing marbles on the lawn with my eight-year-old son on the first day back at training this season. I normally have 200 things going through my mind but all I had to worry about was these marbles."

Neil Warnock on being out of work in the summer

"We are such a young team I'll have a job getting them to bed by nine o'clock. I have a lot of 19 year olds in the squad."

Alan Smith

"It's a St Valentine's Day box of chocolates, one that I am going to enjoy and I hope that when I unwrap, it has got a soft centre."

Iain Dowie on Arsenal's erratic defence... before a 5-1 Valentine's Day loss

"He can play at the back in his suit."

Trevor Francis on Hayden Mullins

"It's been great for me to put the cream on the top of this particular trifle. We've got some nice cream."

Alan Pardew

"Mr Massey says if he's got it wrong he will be suspended for a couple of games. I said to him, 'When you're sat on your settee when you're suspended will you think about us?'"

Neil Warnock

"The assistant Trevor Massey gave a corner instead of a goal kick when the ball had come off Nathan Delfouneso's legs. In the TV interview I said the officials must have thought, 'We don't know which way to give it, so we'll give it to the Premier League team as they are losing.' [My wife] Sharon reminded me that in our game in the previous round Palace had taken the lead against Wolves from a corner that shouldn't have been given."

Neil Warnock

"Their QC asked me what I meant when I said I thought my Observer article was 'pragmatic'? I asked what he thought I meant and the chairman said, 'Answer the question'. I accused the QC of meaningless semantics, so he asked me, 'What do you mean by semantics?' He wasn't joking."

Simon Jordan

"Trying to get the ball off him is very, very hard – he uses that big bum of his very well."

James McArthur on Jason Puncheon

"I am stressed to hell – not when I watch my team, not when I'm out on the grass coaching, but just trying to say 'Who's this? Where has he come from? What's his name? How do you spell it?'"

Ian Holloway

"I have tried to turn things round by giving my players their belief back. Don't be fooled because I wear a Saville Row suit and drink red wine."

Alan Smith

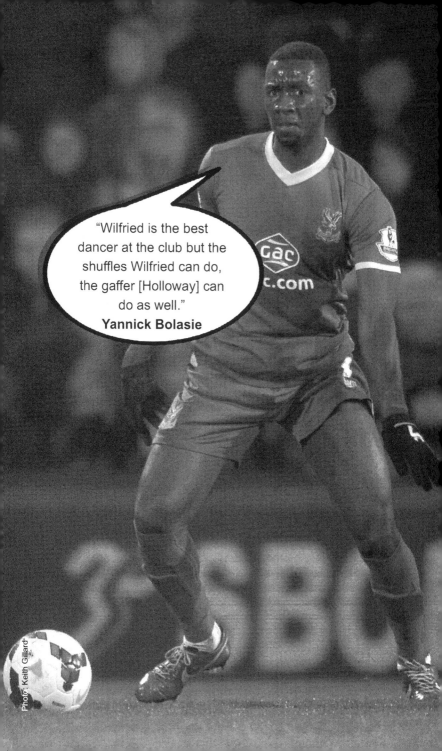

"Harry Redknapp phoned me and said it's the 21st century – how long since we put a man on the moon? And yet FIFA won't let us have cameras on the goalposts?"

Neil Warnock on the Freddie Sears 'ghost goal' at Bristol City

"Gary Johnson is supposed to be a gentleman – unlike myself – and he nodded straight away that it was a goal."

Neil Warnock

"If it happened at Palace I'd offer Bristol City another game, but they are gutless and won't."

Simon Jordan

"The lack of communication is appalling. We've got foreign lads who speak little English and English players who barely speak English."

Alan Smith

"Firstly, I don't see him smiling enough and secondly, he takes everything like a massive disappointment."

Alan Pardew on Wilfried Zaha

"I can't see any faults, I'm sure he has some – you should maybe ask his wife. But even his dress sense is fine by me."

Iain Dowie

"Wilfried Zaha might be out for about six months to stop you from talking about him all the time. Get my message do you? I should hope so. That's probably Arsene Wenger on the phone now. Knowing you lot, it would be and there'll be some sort of story about it. For Christ sakes, write about something else. He's going to be out for months and months. Why should I give you a straight answer? I'm sick and fed up about reading about him. If it happens, it happens, if it don't, it don't. Try and get other stories. And as for your little programme on the telly where you're counting down, just go and get a job, get a life. However many days and however many hours are left till this stupid, pathetic window that forces people to have to do things is just... not very good is it?"

Ian Holloway

"We've bought instant footballers, instant goals and instant ability. It's like putting the milk and butter into the pot to get mashed potatoes."

Bert Head

"I will only leave this club if they carry me out in a dead box."

Sasa Curcic

"Call me ugly... Some people are blessed in looks and some in ability and I think I'm better off with ability so cuss me while I make money."

Wilfried Zaha

"I've changed nappies, I've bathed him twice. He loves me, he cries when everybody else does it, but he knows his dad's buff."

Clinton Morrison

"The good thing about these early kick-offs is that you can go out for a meal and still be in your pyjamas for half eight."

Neil Warnock

"I have often likened a football manager's life to that of a pimp. You depend on other people for your success and are not in control."

Steve Coppell

"Once he got to understand my Scottish accent we got on fine!"
George Burley on Edgar Davids

Photo: Magnus Andersson

"I have to admit it is between England and the Republic. And England is the one I've always dreamed of playing for as a kid."

Clinton Morrison

"My mind was definitely made up when my mother's side of the family, who are all Irish, told me to declare for Mick's team. I'm definitely 100 per cent Irish now. They are all top men over there and it was a very good craic."

Clinton Morrison

"If I'd have been him, I'd have gone down the training ground, said 'thanks lads' and pulled out an AK-47. They hadn't done it for him, but they could beat the champions for Alan Curbishley. F*cking unbelievable."

Simon Jordan on then West Ham boss Alan Pardew

"I keep telling myself too much. Keep your eye on the ball, not on the scoreboard. My rule for the end of the season is 'KISS = Keep It Simple Stupid!'"

Aki Riihilahti

"Why did the referee play four minutes 55 seconds of injury time and not the four minutes that was shown? You've got to ask him, he has refused to see me. They go back to their jobs, referees, and give no thought about professionals like us having to work as hard as we've done tonight. 'So what? It's only a penalty, it's only a goal, it's only an extra minute, I'm enjoying myself'. Dear me, it's disgraceful."

Neil Warnock after Bristol City scored in the fifth minute of stoppage time

"You plan to face the opposition, not the officials. The ref had a bad day at the office and I thought it was a bit out of order for him to punch the air when they scored! I told my players not to shake the referee's hand. A few did because they wanted to talk to him – not through any loving care."

Neil Warnock claims referee Richard Beeby celebrated the injury-time goal against Bristol City

"The local authority became socialist for the first time in 100 years. I had a lot of new local councillors that suddenly started feeling they were representing 24 votes around the corner and became big-time Charlies."

Ron Noades frustrated by Croydon Council's lack of support for building a new Main Stand

"You can ask my wife what time I finish and what time I start. She'll tell you. Last night it was half past 12, watching clips."

Ian Holloway

"I have got nothing to worry about. I can't get sacked because I haven't got a contract and I won't go grey because I am already."
**Caretaker manager
Kit Symons**

"Terry [Venables] saw me coming... He took advantage of a young, inexperienced man with an enthusiasm for football."

Mark Goldberg

"I enjoy playing with these lads, although I don't understand anything what that Scottish striker is talking, he should really learn English."

Aki Riihilahti on Dougie Freedman

"Some of the songs our fans were singing, I found myself chuckling. I can't wait to hear what they come up with on Sunday."

Ian Holloway

"Is he entitled to dance with his wife at a do? Yes he is. Does he need some help with his dance moves? Obviously he does. We will do some more movement to music in training."
Iain Dowie on Andy Johnson

"I think there might be one or two games where I don't get some decisions going for me – from people who have read my book!"
Neil Warnock

"To tell you the truth he's extremely average in training."
Alan Smith on Marco Gabbiadini

"And the question for people like me, and ultimately for Iain, is how in God's name does an agent, whose entire motivation is his own gain, succeed in achieving a divisiveness between the player and club who have had the boy for eight years and looked after his family, given him his opportunity and every encouragement? How does someone like that wield this level of influence over a player?"

Simon Jordan slams Wayne Routledge's agent Paul Stretford

"No footballer of talent should play in the back four."

Malcolm Allison

"I wouldn't say kick in the teeth, it feels a lot worse than that. It probably feels like somewhere else, more like the crown jewels."

Ian Holloway

"I think my half-time team talk did the trick really – I asked [referee Chris Foy] if he wanted some smelling salts, I didn't think the concentration level was good enough from him in the first half."

Neil Warnock

"I feel like a kid who has built a sand castle and has had it knocked over."

Bert Head on leaving Palace

"When I was asked whether I got on with other chairman what I said was, 'It's fair to say that a fair proportion of them are tossers, but
I am pretty sure they think the same thing about me'."

Simon Jordan

"Paddy McCarthy was breathing through his backside after two games in 48 hours."

Neil Warnock

"This is a feather in our cap. It's there in our pocket."

Ian Holloway

"I took them to a hotel last night to keep them away from the New Year celebrations, but there must have been some party going on which I did not know about."

Alan Smith after a 3-0 New Year's Day loss at Millwall

"I can't think of another body of incompetent, senile, decrepit old fogeys who sit in judgement on our national game anywhere in the world!"

Palace director Geoff Geraghty on the FA who allowed Liverpool an early return to Europe in 1991 at the expense of the Eagles

"I was ordered to be baby-sitting the great Ali Benarbia. It is not my ideal football experience but it is part of the job. It is so boring to follow for 90 minutes just one player, especially French speaking. I had to be sharp all the time, even though sometimes when we had the ball, we were just standing on the sidelines looking at chicks from the tribunes."

Aki Riihilahti

"Then Simon Jordan came in and pissed everybody off and we all started to leave!"

Fraser Digby

"One of the problems with black players is I don't think too many can read the game... You get an awful lot with great pace, great athletes, love to play with the ball in front of them, but when it's behind it's chaos... The black players at this club lend the side a lot of skill and flair, but you also need white players in there to balance things up and give the team some brains and some common sense."

Ron Noades

"He was so negative he interfered with the signal strength on my phone."

Simon Jordan on Steve Coppell

"We're not really at the top of the tree when it comes to pizzas in this area but a kebab or a burger would go down well if we got a clean sheet."

Alan Pardew

"I'm just trying to talk in a way so people don't think I'm funny any more, I'm fed up with that. I'm not a comedian, I'm a football manager."

Ian Holloway

"I'm not one for working out the exact figures but we'll need roughly two points a game."

Peter Taylor

"Front line did, the back line did it and they got through us. And my back line did opposite to my middle line. I mean I could have scored that, it's just ridiculous."

Ian Holloway

"I hope they absolutely hammer him. That's what the supporters are there for, be nice to us and out of order to the opposition."

Peter Taylor on Steve Bruce

"Nine months of misery."

Steve Coppell when asked what promotion to the top flight meant for Palace in 1997

"During pre-season, after I'd spent £5m on players, we got beat 5-1 by Crawley, 4-0 by Reading and 6-0 by Millwall! So I had the temerity to ask Steve [Coppell], 'What the f*ck is going on?' And he just said, 'We don't get on, do we?' I agreed and we decided to part company."

Simon Jordan

"I don't think the lad would've had a free header with [Carl] Fletcher on the pitch but he had to rush off because his wife was having contractions. Women can be so inconvenient can't they? It's cost us a bloody point!"

Neil Warnock

"Don't you know who I am? won't get you into nightclubs."
Aki Riihilahti

Photo: Gordon Law

Aki Riihilahti

"November is a useless month. Always dull weather, bad results, small problems and even the girl calendar has a left-over babe on it. December instead is the month full of surprises, fit calendar girls, joy and belief in many things."

"I have lost many people and friends with the disappearance of my SIM card. So if some Juan or Pablo from Portugal answers my number, please tell those bandits that I am struggling. Return my Nokia you b*stards."

MAD ALL OVER

"How can you even call cricket a sport! Isn't it just white upper class fat people trying to have an excuse to get away from their boring homes? So they invented something where you don't need to sweat or do really anything but you can still have a nice cup of tea with your mates in the name of sports."

"I thought it was a bit rude when the umpire gestured me with a finger so I showed my middle one back. There may be a career for me in cricket after football, though it would help if I knew the rules!"

"More bad news: my senior pet cat Lineker has past away. He was a good friend and important family member, God bless his soul."

"I met this girl that had really lovely hair. Wanting to give a compliment to her I expressed my thoughts in a true Londoner way. I never heard from that bird again. Well, I kind of understand it now, after seeing couple of episodes of Ali G."

"It was a bit dim and suddenly I accidentally stepped on dog sh*t. I have done it many times before and it always smells as bad."

"The only thing that bothers me is that some ridiculously looking teammates are moaning about my clothes. Let's face it lads, we are not in the 90s anymore, at this millennium you are allowed to look good. If you wake up you will understand that the jumper was stylish."

"You politicians and journalists are the worst. You are wrong. Your heavy words are too often painted by jealousy. You are just the bloody vegetarian dish in a kebab shop."

"It is quite scary when strangers desperately need to know if you tend to use salt and vinegar with fish and chips."

"Normally when the club sends you to a sportsman's dinner, you go there hoping the chicken wouldn't be too dry this time, that there would be at least one girl on your table and that nobody would come to abuse your team-mates to you."

"I am so exited, I just can't hide it. I am about to lose control and I think like it. Yes, I lost it already. I can't sing this 80s disco hit, although I know the words."

"I always thought swimming was just a light exercise for fat people who didn't really like to sweat. I was wrong."

MAD ALL OVER

"True friends are found out when you play against the big boys. They call you out of the blue, tell you how nice you are and how well you've played in the Premiership, and more importantly, that they are free when you are playing against Man Utd or Arsenal. Didn't hear from them when we were playing Rotherham. They are Premiership friends."

"What Mona Lisa is for every painter and waking up next to Angelina Jolie for every man, playing in the World Cup is for all footballers."

"Someone tried to put their thumb in my arse last week. I've never before experienced such a cruel attack. I was only trying to block the keeper's view standing next to the wall when unexpectedly I was attacked from behind. Luckily the finger was blocked by my shorts."

"I used to be an ugly boy. I remember the times when I tried to get any attention from girls. Usually I got a thin response. It was understandable: I am not actually a Brad Pitt. However now I have suddenly received many Valentine's Day cards, love letters, even panties by post. What is different now is that I have become a footballer."

MAD ALL OVER

"Typical Englishman John Smith is more concerned about David Beckham's fitness than his own wife's. Typical Chinese man Som Young Guy is not trying to grow the population of his country for over one month. Typical German Jurgen wants to check from the map that whereabouts in Europe the cheating Uruguay is located."

"My mind often wonders at the game so I'm not always really there and listening – as we all know women always are!"

"Preparation is boring. Actually, so are footballers – we are not that exciting at all. At least I'm not, although I've been suggested to be a bit of a nutter. I'm just bang on boring most of the times. My highlight of the day on Fridays is to get skinny takeaway cappuccino from Starbucks.

"The other week when I was deep in going through my switch-play options and suddenly another image came to my head – Halle Berry in a jacuzzi. I tried to get myself back giving a long pass, but there she was again, all soaped up. My concentration went."

"Rejection is in the top three of all the humiliating moments in life. Way before not being able to perform with a new girlfriend or congratulating someone for pregnancy when she's just eaten a lot."

"[Soon after arriving in SE25] 'Aki, when you get the ball, remember to bend it straight', was the last advice I got from Steve Kember before the crucial final day game against Stockport. I only understood the paradox when everyone started laughing."

"Every respectable football person has scored a winning goal in the World Cup final. My first was a flying header against Peter Shilton 1982. It went in between the oak tree and gardening table in our back yard."

"My first-ever coach said to me, 'You got to play how you look like, ugly, because that is for you the best way to win – which you have to in this profession.' So I had to leave my bag full of tricks to training ground laughs, school presentations and a possible career in circus after football and turn into midfield enforcer."

"I feel a bit cheated because it's been nine months, yet the story is still the same: I can see from the mirror the same old ugly duckling. The Premiership doesn't make you a beautiful swan."

"[In the Premier League] You can sometimes get Molton Brown body wash with your bath. In the Championship, you were lucky to get warm water and a toilet that didn't smell like last month's Chinese takeaway."

"My life changed quickly, as a nightmare 2003 turned into my best-ever year in 2004. It was like being entertained by Seinfeld straight after watching old replays of Murder She Wrote. And I didn't want to change back to old programmes ever again."

"I heard one female supporter laughing when a big striker scored from a corner that size seems to matter also in football. Not everything though. Movement is equally important, you have to get into the right areas."

Read Aki's diaries at www.akiriihilahti.com

Simon Jordan

On Ron Noades...

"I think he thinks he's sold it [the ground] to some property developers. It was not a false front, someone else goes and buys it for me and I buy it from them. I realise the first bird sh*t that falls on the Holmesdale Stand will be mine to clear up."

"Unfortunately for Ron there are no vacancies at Crystal Palace, but if he wants to send in his CV, I will be happy to take a look at it."

"There were times he [Noades] got so far up my nose I could feel his boots on my chin."
Simon Jordan

"I admit I have bought some players who have been very poor acquisitions, but Ron's record wasn't perfect – look at Marco Gabbiadini for £1.8m or Gareth Taylor for £1.25m."

"Both myself and Ron can be difficult to deal with and both of us can be vitriolic and sometimes contemptuous. I'm not going to be in this instance, I'll leave it to Ron as he's better equipped at that."

"So long as I've got breath in my body, I won't sell this club back to Ron Noades."

"I don't want to be like Ron Noades, hanging around like bad smell, but it was a football club I owned for ten years and I do have views because I'm still passionate about it."

"I have only been in the business three years and cannot profess to know as much as someone like Ron who has done it for 30 years. Of course, Ron would have done things differently, he would not have put his hand in his pocket!"

On Birmingham City...

"My problems with Birmingham started when I went into the boardroom at St Andrew's and David Sullivan came up to me and said: 'Simon, I have known you for a few years but you keep yourself to yourself. Are you gay?'"

"I think in life you get what you deserve. Despite my distaste for the owners, I don't wish any club bad luck. If Birmingham go down, am I going to shed a tear? No. Because the best thing about Birmingham is the road out."

The funniest Crystal Palace quotes... ever!

"I have no problems with Steve Bruce, I like him a lot. I just have an issue with the imbeciles he works for."

"I see other club's chairmen as the enemy. I want to go in there and beat them up. Some of them like Sullivan I would like to do that to."

"I am 6ft 2in, and they're [Sullivan and Gold] both below 5ft 4in, so I'd never see eye to eye with them."

"Birmingham – my favourite club, full of my favourite people."

MAD ALL OVER

"If I see another David Gold interview on the poor East End Jewish boy done good I'll impale myself on one of his dildos."

"Yes, I can empathise with their frustrations: they'd just been beaten 7-0. The fact that I was dancing round the room laughing doesn't mean I can't understand the exasperation."

"I think they are disingenuous. The ethics with which they do business, I don't appreciate. I have had enough dealings with them to be able to have that view. Am I surprised? They sell dildos for a living. That gives you a judgement on what they may or may not be."

"David Sullivan says he resents his players and their salaries. Fair enough. Respect, likeability, decency – it all matters. Birmingham's players should look at David: £575m made out of open-leg porn mags, chatlines, sex dolls, an ISP offering 'furry fuckers' and 'anal frenzy', movies like Hellcats: Mud Wrestling and Star Sex, all run from an £18m mansion in Essex. What's not to like about that?"

"Gold and Sullivan are bizarre. I'm not saying I'm perfect, that I'm a self-effacing wallflower, but being an owner just isn't as hard as they make it."

"I am a man who shakes hands on a deal and keeps his word – I don't know if they are. Steve Bruce and Birmingham deserve one another."

On Charlton Athletic...

"The only reason I'd buy Charlton is so I could close it down. I don't like the way their board operates. I don't like the way Richard Murray conducts himself, I don't like the way their fans conduct themselves. It's not my favourite place and they are not my favourite fans or favourite club. They should be extremely grateful Palace gave them a ground to play at 15 years ago."

"I don't enjoy seeing anyone struggle because I think that if you wish ill on people then it comes back on you. I don't wish relegation on Charlton, I don't wish anything on Charlton – I have a level of disinterest."

"Charlton have a cheap match-day coach service that goes out into Kent to nick Gillingham fans – that's pretty clever. We might start sending a coach to Brighton."

"I remember seeing [Charlton chief] Richard Murray in court when I took Iain Dowie to court. The next time I talk to Richard Murray will be through a medium."

"I couldn't care less about Charlton. They're a bunch of nobodies. They spread lies about me. Rotten, dirty lies. When they didn't have a ground, we gave them ours. Yet when we get relegated in the last minute at The Valley, their fans do a conga? Their chairman turns around to me and says, 'Enjoy The Championship... t*sser.' That's just despicable."

"Charlton's fans revelled in it, abused us and even did the bloody conga. In retrospect, of course I regret calling them morons. Imbeciles would have been more appropriate."

On Iain Dowie...

"They think they are the rocket man because they've got a degree in rocket science. Nonsense. Some of the stupidest people I have met in my life are people who have got degrees and if he believes his own hype, he will come undone."

"If you are lied to and somebody is trying to leg you over by getting out of a contract to their own advantage and tells you bear-faced lies, and turns up at the very place he said he wasn't going to go, are you going to be worried about good feeling between yourselves?"

"I would not issue a writ through my lawyers on a point of principle, I will issue it on a point of law because a point of principle is expensive, as Iain will find out."

"He's a big boy and takes responsibility for his actions. He took decisions to make representations to me and the consequences are his to bear."

"I didn't get any satisfaction from [Dowie's] demise at Charlton, instead I gained a great deal of satisfaction from smashing him to pieces in court."

"I agreed a deal for Michael Carrick while he was at West Ham, but he wouldn't even return Iain Dowie's calls, but I can understand that because I wouldn't return Dowie's calls either."

"I don't want to say it, because I hated our manager at the time. I didn't like him at all. His manners, outlook and attitude stank. And I told him so, after we won the play-off final. So what he got promotion? That's what I paid him to do."

[When asked whether Dowie was appealing the verdict of their court case] "There's nothing appealing about Iain Dowie!"

Jordan on celebrity culture...

"I hate the modern day celebrity where people are getting recognised for doing absolutely nothing, achieving absolutely nothing and being absolutely vile. People like Jordan are absolute garbage."

"If you end up on I'm A Celebrity... or Celebrity Love Island you should be insulted. Who are these people? It just makes me laugh. None of them has a pot to piss in, or any talent. If celebrity means being Jade Goody I want obscurity."

The funniest Crystal Palace quotes... ever!

"Wayne [Rooney] doesn't need advice on gambling. His mistakes in the past two years have been overblown, and he's maturing. If the Queen can punt her b*llocks off, as they say in the trade, why can't Wayne?"

"Quite a few teachers from my day were still there, and they all said, 'We always knew you were going to be successful'. What a load of rubbish! I remember one year my school report said: 'Simon has set himself a very low standard this year... and failed to achieve it'."

Printed in Poland
by Amazon Fulfillment
Poland Sp. z o.o., Wrocław

51125528R00114